TOWARD MORNING
SELECTED POEMS

TOWARD MORNING
SELECTED POEMS

BRUCE BOYD

EDITED BY BILL MOHR

MAGRA BOOKS
LOS ANGELES BAGNONE
2026

Magra Books

The publisher has tried all means at their disposal to establish the estate of Bruce Boyd and the rights to the work therein, and is surely disposed to account for those rights, if any such person or persons should come forward.

Introduction © 2026 Bill Mohr. All rights reserved.

Design by S. E. Pessin

Order from IngramSpark and www.magrabooks.com

S. E. Pessin & Paul Vangelisti, co-editors

magrabooks.com
magrabooks@gmail.com
PRINTED IN THE USA
ISBN 979-8-9926955-1-9

This book is dedicated to Harley W. Lond.

CONTENTS

Introduction

Bruce Boyd: Poète Perdu of Donald Allen's *The New American Poetry*   11

Part I

The Actual Flesh Is Simple Breath Without a Voice	21
After Midnight	22
Aubade	23
Scratching	24
This Is How the Wind Sings, Lover, on the Beach	26
A Quarrel of Minstrels	27
Water	28
Song	29
Poem	30
Summer Nightmusic	31
N O W	34
Sanctuary	35
This Is What the Watchbird Sings, Who Perches in the Lovetree	36
Venice Recalled	37

Part II

Flowerpot Sutra	41
Canticles for the Hours: Prime	50
Thread	54

Part III

Introduction	61
Proem	62
Toward Morning (Some Apotropeia Instead of an Alba)	63
Envoy, with Angelic Orders	71

Chronological Order of Publication
Note on the Editor

BILL MOHR

INTRODUCTION

INTRODUCTION

BRUCE BOYD: POÈTE PERDU OF DONALD ALLEN'S *THE NEW AMERICAN POETRY*

Donald Allen's anthology of "underground" poets, *The New American Poetry* (Grove Press, 1960), was no different from any other book issued by a publisher with the profit margin in mind: it had been to be marketed, and Allen knew full well that the best advertisement for his project would be to make the contents seem as much of an outlier as possible: the poems in his anthology, he claimed, exuded a total rejection of academic poetry. His introduction, as I pointed out in *Hold-Outs: The Los Angeles Poetry Renaissance 1948-1992*, slightly exaggerated the contrast between *NAP* and the academic poets in such anthologies as *New Poets of England and America*. On a quick glance, it did seem to be a stark binary, in which those who practiced traditional versification appeared in institutional magazines, whereas experimental poets found their legitimation in coterie magazines with little capital to support them other than sheer editorial endeavor. In point of fact, several poets in *NAP* had appeared in *Poetry* magazine, which was about as established a magazine as one could aspire to appear in in mid-century America; and one only had to read a portion of Jack Spicer's contribution to *NAP* to realize that iambic pentameter had not exactly vanished from the playbook of poets in *NAP*.

Aided by this marketing sleight-of-hand, the eminent success of Allen's anthology generated far more aftershocks that simply giving much deserved attention to poets on both coasts of the United States whose work was primarily appearing in magazines that did not have wide circulation. For one thing, Allen subsequently expanded *NAP* into a sequel that did not include all of the original contributors. Among those not included in the revised edition in 1982 was Bruce Boyd, the only poet in *NAP* never to have had even a chapbook of his poetry published.

It needs to be emphasized that whenever I have brought up this anomaly during the past 25 years, even poets and critics who think of themselves as exceptionally well-informed about mid-20th century poetry blink in puzzled recollection. "Oh," they say, as if a single syllable of retrospective disbelief sufficed to requite this aporia, and then — because they have suddenly realized they don't know Allen's anthology as impeccably as they thought they did — change the topic of conversation. I can't say I blame them for feeling slightly chagrined. I, too, for several decades overlooked a poet whose work appeared alongside canonical poets in several of the most prestigious "underground" outlets of that period: *Evergreen Review, Yugen, Floating Bear,* and the legendary *J: A Magazine of Poetry.* One might think it's almost impossible to be a notable part of the literary history of that period and remain utterly neglected, but Boyd's lack of any individual title demonstrates that merit alone does not suffice to keep one present in the literary conversation.

As an initial remedial gesture, therefore, this volume is meant to bring together the bulk of the poems that earned Boyd, in his lifetime, the respect of an unusual combination of poets, for Boyd also has the distinction of being the only figure in Jack Spicer's circle in the Berkeley Renaissance to have also been a mid-century member of another significant cluster of poets, the Venice West scene headed up by *NAP* contributor Stuart Z. Perkoff in the 1950s. Extending the obliqueness of Boyd's scalene triangle of associates is yet another representative figure, Gary Snyder, who was not just a fellow contributor to *NAP,* but also one of Boyd's correspondents.

Born in 1928, in San Francisco, Bruce Boyd attended the University of California, Berkeley and at some point encountered Jack Spicer, as well as other poets such as George Stanley and Robin Blaser. Boyd seems not to have started writing poems until he was 22 years old, but he was earnestly circulating his work by the time he moved to the Ocean Park section of Santa Monica in 1953. The Venice West scene of poets had just barely begun to coalesce, and after Boyd met Stuart Z. Perkoff on the beach one night, he began sharing his poems with other poets who were gathering in each other's houses. If Boyd was ensconced in the Venice West scene enough to earn a citation in the roll call of poets on a tape recording in the Lawrence Lipton archive at the University of Southern California, his self-exile from day-to-day contact with the Spicer circle had not caused Spicer to lose respect for his work. In fact, it was Spicer, in 1957, who first brought Boyd to Donald Allen's attention. We know this because Allen wrote to Boyd on August 6, and requested that Boyd send him two poems, "Hybris" and "Petition," which he said Spicer had shown him copies of.

How much this interest by Allen, prompted by Spicer's enthusiasm, might have motivated Boyd to return to San Francisco is unknown, but it is the case that by the spring of 1958, Boyd had resettled in the Bay Area and joined a dozen other poets in the Wednesday night poetry workshop that was being led by Robert Duncan at the San Francisco Public Library. This workshop, which Spicer took part in, mirrored his own groundbreaking and notorious "Poetry as Magic" workshop the previous year at the downtown library.

Notably, as Boyd is turning 30 years-old, he was accorded the honor of a full-length reading at the San Francisco Poetry Center, an occasion he used to provide a chronological survey of his favorite poems, including one about Wittgenstein alluded to in a letter by Perkoff to Allen as a "masterpiece." Six months after the reading in San Francisco, which was attended by Jack Spicer, one of Boyd's poems appeared in issue number six of the *Evergreen Review*. In the same year that Boyd appeared in the *Evergreen Review*, he signed a two-page contract with Donald Allen and Grove Press to give permission to have three of his poems appear in an anthology that would sweep many of the poets in the Hall-Pack-Simpson anthology out to the open water of free verse with an overpowering swiftness akin to a cultural riptide.

The most important of Boyd's poems in *NAP* is "Venice Recalled," which I have written about in *Hold-Outs*. I will simply reiterate that Boyd compares and contrasts two communities of poets: that of the Berkeley and San Francisco Renaissance and the community he coalesced with in Venice, and that he found the latter to be more congenial in accommodating his own poetics. This might come as a surprise to many people, given that San Francisco's scenes and movements are usually perceived as the most buoyant and pervasively giddy about its community's valorization of poetry. Written during one of his sojourns in San Francisco — hence the title, "Venice Recalled" — this poem in *NAP* unexpectedly gives the nod to the Southern California scene as being more organically coordinated in its intermingling of the community's environment, domestic life, and the poem as the cynosure of a gift exchange economy.

"Venice Recalled" is not the only retrospective assessment that Boyd ended up providing about his decision to move, in the spring of 1958, from Venice back to San Francisco. In a letter he wrote to Gary Snyder after he had returned to Venice in 1960, he reflected on how fortuitous his departure from Venice West two years earlier had been. Up until 1958, the scene in Venice was still based on the domestic model that was described in Richard Candida Smith's *Utopia and Dissent*. One has only to consult Stuart Z. Perkoff's long letter to Donald Allen in 1959 to corroborate Boyd's account of an organic community in "Venice Recalled."

Other alignments with the Beat ethos also buttress Boyd's peripheral convergence with more prominent figures in mid-century "underground" poetry on the West Coast. Boyd's interest in Zen Buddhism, however, appears to have been particular to him among the Venice West poets. "Flowerpot Sutra," which is dated from 1956, is unlike any other Beat-associated poem from the middle of the decade. Though the title might seem to echo Ginsberg's "Sunflower Sutra," it has no other overlap with that well-known early poem by Ginsberg. While Kerouac's *Dharma Bums* was written that same year, it wasn't published until two years later; Boyd, in fact, had no contact with Kerouac or Ginsberg that I have been able to verify. By chance, D.T. Suzuki's essay on Zen was published in the same issue of *Evergreen Review* in which Boyd had his poem "Aubade," but Suzuki's essay could hardly be said to be the inspiration for Boyd's commitment to early morning meditation sessions in San Francisco.

Boyd's decision to move back to Los Angeles in the early 1960s was probably due to economic considerations. He had been working in a bookstore with Joanne Kyger in San Francisco, but that kind of employment would only have permitted very austere accommodations. As he noted in his long letter to Snyder in 1960, until he returned to Venice, he did not even live in a situation in which he had his own bathroom. The "scene" in Venice, unfortunately, was in the process of collapse. If the poets who had first gathered in each other's houses in the mid-1950s had envisioned an enclave in which they could nurture an organic, multi-disciplinary habitat, then this had been washed away in part because of Lawrence Lipton's best-selling book, *The Holy Barbarians*, which single-handedly generated a massive influx of Beat wannabes to Venice, in the same way that popular music served as an alluring conduit for runaway teenagers of the hippie generation to show up in the Haight-Asbery in the summer of 1967. Venice West also imploded due to the decision of poets such as Stuart Z. Perkoff to become addicted to heroin, which ultimately led to his imprisonment in the mid-1960s.

Unusual for a poet associated with two different scenes on the West Coast, Boyd then became involved with political activity, including writing articles for a radical, local newspaper in Venice called *The Spectre*, which was edited by John Haag, the eventual co-founder of the Peace & Freedom party. By 1964, Boyd was working with CORE (Congress of Racial Equality) and found himself on trial for a misdemeanor related to an act of civil disobedience. His constant struggle to find steady work that paid decently finally appears to have worn him down by 1965, at which point he began to study computer programming and was hired to write computer code for the County of Los Angeles.

Boyd ceased to communicate with literary magazines and wrote Donald Allen that he was not writing any new poetry and was focused instead on his job. He had not had any book of his work published by that point: not even a 16 page chapbook, and it does not seem as if he made any effort to get one published, even though a poet with his record of publication should have had no trouble getting a collection into print. Does this lack of a stand alone collection of his poems represent Boyd's idiosyncratic preference; or did he simply refuse to pursue publication beyond appearances in a magazine? Or was he open to having a collection published, but didn't feel comfortable with the social process of soliciting even a small press publisher? It's not unusual for a person working at the avant-garde margins of culture to feel that the literary hustle is a zero sum game, and Boyd may well have felt a justifiable disdain for such egotistic gamesmanship. "I don't have a lot of money riding on them," Boyd said about his poems when he first met Perkoff and showed him some poems.

In any case, this book marks the first time Boyd's poems have appeared in a stand-alone volume. The title was chosen as a result of a note by Diane di Prima about contributors to *The Floating Bear* in which she said that the poems she was publishing came from a manuscript entitled *Toward Morning: An Apotropeia instead of an Alba*, "probably written in the late 1950s." The complete manuscript has not been found in any archive. My decision on the contents of this book is a simple default: focus on the poems published in magazines and in *New American Poetry*. That arrangement will at least allow readers to gain an appreciation of his work similar to the esteem his comrades and friends might have had by subscribing to the magazines most frequented by the avant-garde at that time. Let us remember that between 1958 and 1961, Boyd's poems appeared in several of the best known underground magazines of the period: *Evergreen Review*, *Floating Bear*, *Yugen*, and Jack Spicer's legendary "*J*" magazine.

In suggesting this contextual perspective, I would urge readers to examine issue number seven (1961) of *Yugen* magazine, edited by LeRoi Jones and Hettie Cohen, as indicative of Boyd's inclusion among his peers the year after *NAP* appears. Even a quick glance at the list of that issue's contributors should enable anyone to understand why critic Stephen Belletto ranks *Yugen* as "the most important Beat-associated magazine" of that period. The phrase "beat-associated" is a crucial aspect of this categorization, for the most efficacious little magazines affiliated with mid-century avant-garde poetry were particularly interested in generating networks of writers with affinities for coteries other than their own. One can see the capaciousness of this dynamic in the following alphabetized list of contributors (in addition to Jones) to the seventh issue of *Yugen*: John Ashbery; Bruce Boyd; Gregory Corso; Robert Creeley; Diane DiPrima; Larry Eigner; Max Finstein; Allen Ginsberg; Kenneth Koch; Edward Marshall; Frank O'Hara; Charles Olson; Joel Oppenheimer; Stuart Z. Perkoff; Gilbert Sorrentino; George Stanley; and Philip Whalen. Among the issue's stellar moments is the first publication of O'Hara's classic manifesto, "Personism." Boyd is the third contributor in order of actual presentation in this issue, with his "6 Poems" following Jones and Sorrentino in the table of contents. With *NAP* and *Yugen* No. 7 striding hand-in-hand down avant-garde avenue, one could hardly ask to be in better company two years in a row.

That this book is being published by a literary project overseen by Paul Vangelisti can hardly be called a coincidence. Stuart Z. Perkoff and John Thomas, two of the poets associated with Venice West, had several volumes published by Red Hill Press. Nor is Vangelisti alone in excavating this portion of West Coast poetry. In the middle of the last decade, I was the editorial mentor for another member of that scene, Eileen Aronson Ireland, whose work was admired by both Perkoff and Thomas. Finally, it should be pointed out that Boyd's sojourns between Northern and Southern California were hardly unique to him as a member of Venice West. Both Perkoff and Thomas spent several years in Northern California after the collapse of Venice West. If Vangelisti and I have insisted on a comprehensive canon of antinomian continuity, it is in part because the poets of Venice West have long deserved the same place at the table that they earned with their appearance in *The New American Poetry*. Boyd is the quintessential maverick poet on the West Coast between 1950 and 1965, but his ability to forestall a reckoning with his work has come to an end. Maria Damon once commented that no one can live at the margins forever. In being a peripatetic friend of Jack Spicer, Robin Blaser, Donald Allen, Stuart Z. Perkoff, Gary Snyder, and Joanne Kyger, Bruce Boyd has tested that deflection with supreme dexterity. I leave it to those who admire the individuals I just named, as friends of Boyd, to begin assessing the work of a poet that intermingled all of them in the alembic of poetry.

    Bill Mohr
    Long Beach, California
    October, 2025

BRUCE BOYD

PART I

PART I

THE ACTUAL FLESH IS SIMPLE BREATH WITHOUT A VOICE

the actual flesh is simple breath without a voice.
like snakes that make their season's nest in hollow trees
we shed our skin before its death & live by choice.

the words we have to speak can serve as a device
to warm us at a distance: but in the closer heat we freeze.
the actual flesh is simple breath without a voice,

& words, to us who wish to love, seem too precise:
their itch demands a scratch; but hands that scratch displease.
we shed our skin before its death & live by choice.

among the gestures that we have to choose: which are concise
as sudden open doors & startled eyes & quickly rigid knees.
the actual flesh is simple breath without a voice.

the snake that eats its tail lacks right advice:
it saves its skin but finds the flesh it has to nibble disagrees;
we shed our skin before its death & live by choice.

to breathe & not to say a word might be to rejoice;
the eye sees only shadows made by names until it sees
the actual flesh is simple breath without a voice
we shed our skin before its death & live by choice.

July 1958

AFTER MIDNIGHT

      the pumpkin landed upside down,
      the little light went out behind its eyes.
      a glass of wine before the sound of mice
      divided silence from the music
      shattered, as they scurried to the willows

I am forgetting the words, even for the simplest things
there is no power in words, no power at all
      to fill a glass of water
& come at night to pour the moon across your hands.

AUBADE

While the sea-bird rises / with the moon,
flinging dry sand / into the eye of the mountain,
moonrise, stinging the cricket's eye, moistens the room, unties

the light-stiff latch of the word-strung wicket.   Out flies
the moon-bird, flies to the top of the bright wet mountain
to sing. Words, prized by the cricket, drop from the moon-

bird's beak like beads unstrung from a string. Words / pass,
rattle for a while in recollection. Words / leave recollection.
Recollection greets the wordless sunrise, dry;

meets it with a sound of greeting / like a sigh, as
a bone-dry fountain might / gasp a waterless deception
up to where the birds fly by.

Blown back, then (along with the moon,
recollection waits with the cricket
for moonrise, again / & the sea-bird to moisten the room.

SCRATCHING

the poems that they make in hell are done with mirrors
used for traps & names like little tinkly bells for bait.
they raise up against the ways of my destruction.
closed songs: feedback in the isolated system:
precision in inches: measurement without direction.
      so you understand:
      so i've given myself away:
& it's all done with mirrors. a game for shut-ins,
played in the smokey light, painful & useless,
                            i mean
      LET ME OUT.

look, i'm going to throw my bait out with the twigs & seeds,
these are the portions the big cats reject, look

    the head of a squeezy snake in moult,
    sly birds in hooded cages (i could like a bird like this
by now no more than Tobit could),
    rank leaves & pickled roots from trees dug out of stumps,
    statues of invented angles,
    jacks-in-the-box & also jacks in the basket,
    knives & other tools for mumbleypeg,
    knucklebones & little rubber balls,
    brassy old clappers from towers,
    the bodies of the mice that ate my stash last summer
then kicked their little frames,
    irene tavener with a bandolier of rubber ashtrays;
festoons, & paper rosettes
with this last & stuffiest quotation, "one alone is the real, the wise
call it by many names", this means the main wheel turns
with ease on many little bearings
with ease on many little bearings
                        but the mouth of the river
devours the thread of the water /
                    & watch this garbage

move across the smoothness of it, shifting
in & out of patterns, changing
                         towards the centre to a powder,
                              dropping /
whatever you have there, drop it. *Drop it.*
DROP IT.

COME & LET ME OUT NOW /
    I'M TIRED & DIRTY & I WANT TO TAKE A BATH.

(1958)

THIS IS HOW THE WIND SINGS, LOVER, ON THE BEACH

beloved,
I cd never / be the sky
but I / cd be the weather

on top of the waves
on top of the water, lover
come dance with me, & draw
me, lover, together

    and the eyes of all the other / dancers
    follow us,
    and the arms of all the other swimmers
    swim to us

A QUARREL OF MINSTRELS

I think, as the first rain of the season falls
down soft on the street, & the silence grows thin
in the rooms of my friends, & in mine,

how the underbelly of kindness
gives in to fear like a man's skin
gives in the shove of a shiv, so

quiet, & so quick; whose skin
gives in right away to fear, which makes love
collapse in a corner

like a partner who's poked a hot shot, or shatter
like a spinster might shatter a plate.
& it is late; & the silence is damp;

& now the silence will end,
in the rooms of my friends, & in mine.
now the talk will begin,

& the air will rush into our room, from outside;
& it will expand puffed up by the heart of our separate prides,
comparing each other in speech, & rise

& grow
over our heads.

WATER

only the water is strictly just,
for it storms on the face of the water, only;
the deep of the water is stormless.

in the deep of the water, submerged
in its breathless nod, we waken.

the ocean, that thickens our movements
with sense, draws us down to the floor to dance,
humming her terrible senseless songs.

SONG

in the forest of great delight,
do not the spring of the bough, & the leaf,
shaken, exhibit the Thou entire?

they do: entire & instinct, the song
of the bough & the leaf springs
into the long dimension of night.

but we inhabit the forest of fright,
where song is a fang, sinking,
& song is a friend, stinging again,
& the song to be sung is a snarling thread

until singing. then song is dry land in the flood
that ripples inside of the head;
& song is like thread
in the blood.

POEM

the white is for inaccessibility in light.

the red is not for blood. red birds flutter
   in the bare tree that reason the turnings
   of the light or the dark.

the black is for inaccessibility in dark.
watchers,
the birds fly away when you cut the tree down.

SUMMER NIGHTMUSIC

1.

blue-green in twilight, with the moon
comes the sea-bird now,
springing from the middle of the river to

enlist & arm responses; & downstream to sea-mist, through
responsive word-spun shallows, moves / the moon-bird, mobilized, how
it seeks by clinging / on the outside of the river to
keep / clear of the grasping midde, not / now
hearing it sing

      "soon gone, all birds;
      "not recognized until by recollection,
      "then mummified in words.

2.

which having heard,
the wind & the river / conferred;
& the water & weather,
coming together,
said

      "moon-grown / overhead, the birds
      "blown motionless above the blue-green sea, are
      "by sight, seen latticed through the words

      "in flight. the grass-grown birds,
      "blown motionless above the blue-green sea, are
      "clustered / like a moon that waits for words."

3.

watch the moon that flings dumb birds

across the sky at night
foster recollection,

& the green gross carry the song the birds sing
brightly / underneath the moon, as thoughts, blown
room, grown into recollection, can

while the intertwining strands
grasp / tightly their connexion,
& the moon glows singly, like silence from a pair of hands.

4.

now the solitary moon-bird's
sudden sea-prone wings
skim the grasping middle of the river as its sings

"alone / the stalks of sea-grass hang / parted by quiet, as
"water & weather (how the wind & the river, coming together, sang)
    were parted by sound, echoing moon-blows, as the foam-damp
    ground,
"shaking recollection / like a sound shakes idel hands.

"aground in silence where the sands / pass
"back & forth, erasing mountains, can
"the moon / sow back the night, to find protection."

"its black inside the white
"afterglow of night / entails detection;
"but planted, would it germinate, expand?

5.

"intimations glimmer / wave-like   on the day-bright sand.
    play back / & forth, across the line from / recollection to
        projection.
"restive in the middle of the river, I look for swarms of birds
    writing words down / on the line projected onto recollection

as if from verse (which is a woman) onto man;

"words / turn, will the planted moon-bloom grow, seeded with / the
 mountain-grass?

"if birds still fly / above the water; if the stone-cold sand
 turns warm, & the thicket flowers into speech.
"then, renewed, the clustered night will reach the sky in all directions,

6.

    "& be / blown back
    "to wait with
    "the cricket,

"who sings, welcoming the black
"face of moon, responsive with new laughter
"in the word-blown thicket, —

"— if the moon-warmed sand will bloom;
"if the bloom-boned bird, singing in the room
"will plant the moon-stoned sound,
"& if it be / blown back,
"singing like the moon sings, to the cricket,
"waiting;)
  then the bird-blown thicket
"will have flowered like a plan
       (if, blown back,
"singing come the sea-bird."

N O W

so far)

like rain on a slope too long a time dry
heard at night, now the turn comes,
                                   or felt
like former wars to set a bad peace back to rights,
with such delight, comes on
                                        like a flood
of time to a place that knows what to do once again
makes this to greet it

        or her
    the presence of whose grace I mean unfolds
    or seems to disenfold as if there were
    superior dimensions to the place, more light
    across the flood to follow to our lady of

 whom there is nothing to hold to
: for the water subsides.   the afterflood of silt
sloughs off the land in flakes, & dries
& crumbles to a dust that daylight brushes
where the air expands across the field   and half lays bare
this crust of bricks, that spread of bones, a heap of ash
      a perfect dig.

      shall I cultivate these ruins?" to himself
      the learned gardener says.

& a city springs to the eye.

(XII.59)

SANCTUARY

because the warm honey
        is never dissolved, by water,
but drifts on the river's stone bottom
like wads of raw silk,

under the surface the swimmers still look

    where sharp little stars
            bloom on the bone-tree
    & tender incredulous fish
            swim out of its watery eyes

& grow warmer, while gently the bone-tree
        is turned in its bed
    & see how it gradually wakens

around it the water is still:
but the sheet-glass surface is quietly shaken
& breaks into ripples, as gulls rise
into the room of the hungry children
to watch the tall water close over their heads.

1958

THIS IS WHAT THE WATCHBIRD SINGS, WHO PERCHES IN THE LOVETREE

Who has but dighted his tricks in a bed,
And never delighted in anything said,
He'll nibble dry leaves until he is dead.

For love is the kind of a tree whose fruit
Grows not on the branches, but at the root.

Who with his lover's real presence has talked,
And enacted his lover's least speakable thought,
He will find out what it is he has sought.

For love is the kind of a tree whose fruit
Grows not on the branches, but at the root.

1957

VENICE RECALLED

on the salt water streets
that rose & then fell with the ocean
when the fish that were caught in the mud
underneath the wooden footbridge started in to stink,
soon there was always the incoming tide

                                                    there, we were
each his own man

    to speak, the play of sounds, pleasant or
    otherwise, but only open & discursive

                differently, here, at the language
  the oblique sense of a word to stamp one as "in"
                            whose dialect (not
dialectic) held
        "right or wrong"
invents a greater crime that just to force the song:
to force it back,
        & closets them wet & huddled together.

    they are fearful in their heads
    of being on the outside looking in
    — to the center of language

but we who would live openly are its natural peripheries,
& take the unborn where the dead leave it
to grow, at our hand

"always to prefer the common," thus the noble
Heraclitus, in "this world, which is the same for all

    our language is although induction
    the topology of what we live:
    thus not its substitute but its enlargement.

                                    there, with us

a new poem was something
                            the making, something
that asked to be shared at once: seldom a "result"
to praise or blame, & never this only, we mostly looked
behind it for the ways that came together,
between whom, intended, a clearing was being made

in which to discover what, having forgotten
is recovered
            in measure, apart from direction:
    as in accord with old codes,
    codices,
            a kind of love
of least action in language, or
                            taken as return
to the origin,
    a place of actual
welcome, always the nearest
                    stone path that is watered
                    against the coming of guests
        is to say,
                cooler:
& the poem, what it means to say,
for the natural motion of its body, is the clearer
that remarks the wider movement of its actual thought.

1959

BRUCE BOYD

PART II

PART II

FLOWERPOT SUTRA

"One day Buddha was about to preach a sermon. He lifted up a golden lotus flower and without saying a word showed it to the assembled monks. Among them only Mahakasyapa understood. He looked at Buddha and smiled." — Sokei-An, in *Cat's Yawn*

BEGINNING

to begin.   to begin
now.   to live.

to begin to move.

      not in the direction of moving.
      not in the direction of being-moved.

      in the direction of moving-&-being-moved.

      in the direction of not-moving-&-not-being moved.

out.   & in.

are there things to do?
there are things to be done.
there is nothing to be done.   *Oh*
see this flower.   &
smile.

for this, is a way.
it cannot be spoken.
what can be spoken
are places.
to pass.
before.
it.

before the way that is the end of going about.
while being shown
the flower

before seeing.   it.
until.   it.
the smile.

until the then when
I shall see that now
was also that then.

& smile.

this I know having read
it in books,
to begin.

MIDDLE PART

1.

"on!" cry the teachers, "on to the shore!"
over the river's the opposite shore!
you've been there before!
                before!
                    before! and!   what!
was the face that you wore there before?"

        the teachers lean on their staffs, & implore
you to answer & tell them the face that you wore
on the opposite shore, before.
    their voices, words unwobbling
in the vibrant air,
do not, particularly, care
if anymore is there
to listen.
    in them, is nothing that they mean
but do not know they mean:
what one thinks they mean, they mean,
& more.   &, so long as there is / ore,
the voice will implore

& get misunderstood.

but / I
       do not know
               any / buddhas:
I take my unlaid evenings' ends
to the dialectic houses of my friends,
& grow,
    slow by the magic
    of that connatural human love
    which, like the speechless very texture
    of perception, is a fact
    but no one's recreation,
humanly articulate.

our voices, weaving words
between us in the solid air,
show our pain, that we must care
    lest no one, or, again
    lest someone, should be there
to listen.
in them, is everything we mean
    & do not know we mean
    & do not wish to mean
    & know we must not mean:

&,   there are times
when all these possibilities of meaning
    these devious things, nowhere
    completely recorded,
unquiet me, & wake
me to the urgent human terror
that always flutters, gently
in the bottoms of my brain:
when, if people tried to talk to me,
all the words they said would whistle & make echoes
in my head, & all their different meanings threaten me

like weapons, & change the crooning terror
to a paralyzing keen: SOMETHING
                SOMETHING
                SOMETHING
                is
                GOING
                GOING
                GOING
                to
                HAPPEN
                HAPPEN
                HAPPEN

&. I. do. not. move.
not move: lest at the furthest limits
            of a world turned inside out
I find unthinkably a captive, crouching & entrapped,
furtive in brainpan's / unguessable crevice,
immobilized penitent, frantic but passive,
powerless witness / at window to world
that wobbles & wavers / as runaway golden
accomplishment-body / whirls
in a frenzy
              the self,
                      all nude / & out of its role
gulping for air in ultimate corner;
                    panting, & not in control.

but, consider /
    turn, in ultimate corner turn
      & gaze at the wall:
is not, after all,
this, in a sense,
what always
is so?

      for to plain noetic intellection
there are in fact no actors: only acts,
& what we name our selves
are nonexistent / strangers
in the mansions of what process we consist in,
nowhere palpable in marrow, bone, or flesh or skin:
undiscovered when we sit or stand or walk about or sleep:
and, in our thought, when once we stop to think we find
no thinker, only thoughts.
O, we
      who are / as children   / to the very children
are in fact like houses, whose enormous wings
are haunted by a bogeyman.

2.

there is a question
to discuss.
its proper answer is,
to show it answerless:
not knowing what the question is
    (it never was)
not hearing what the answer was
    (speechless like a blanket, &
    it always is)
to cut. / our large & vague discomfort into parts
    (which cannot be)
& worry at the parts like dogs at meatless bones,
for marrow long dried out.

3.

there is
      (& there is known to be
at the turning centre. / of that unmoving room
      (I have talked about madness

where the urgent terrors   / loom expectantly & still
              (& now am talking of love
such a thing as one
              (by learning & by skill
might form a magic circle of, & summon
              (by going from not loving
from the populous bleak houses
              of the dead & dying *it*,
              (to loving
to its waiting incompleteness / possible & living *you*
              (in to being loved.

for this,   the ritual act & incantation
are immanent in need,
       that radically human fact,
       the need we have of our completion,
whereof the art
       (we do not know the needed part
must be / to recognize its signs
& then
       though all its signs are shared
       with something else, & one in fact
       is never undeceived
perform the possibly effective act
& like a shaman, chant the act's
appropriate cantations.
       for the shaman, too
depends on signs   / & sets the times
for acts of magic
           perhaps by noting / flight of bird
           its tiny voice / That he has heard
& like us, by need;
but / the shaman has more art
           the legends of his craft, that language
           of the natural marks of things,
           he knows

than we, who are, by need
mostly misdirected   / In looking out for signs:
& while his rituals
        perplexingly effectual
astonishingly satisfy,
our ineffective ritual declines
to rote, becomes habitual gesture
of impatience & relief,
ambivalent & brief,
& we forget what was the chief
reason that we do it for

O marrow, bone, & flesh, & skin,
let copulation be. / a conjuring for intercourse,
an act, thought problematical,
of sympathetic magic.

& what is problematical in love is how it spreads
its hungry & interrogating threads
all over in the body, like the brain;
how the famished questions that it asks,
        to which the amatory ritual has
        to give a semblance, or,
        the living body
of an answer, will
    unless somehow replied to
comprise themselves a mournful / incantation that at last
will summon up the shadows of a more-than-individual past
to fill the heavy air /   of our unformulated need:
an obscure surly crowd that has us
prowl the reasoned streets
& tense in rented beds & howl,
or guides us
    out of individual life
forgetful to the houses of the dead.

but consider: need shows itself as a relation

from a *me* that is, onto one that isn't;
& one is not. / somewhere *between*,
but takes one's stand in the relation:

for there is
        (& there is known to be
at the whirling fulcrum   / of that unbudging room
        (I have talked   / at names & forms
within whose really incandescent gloom
        the objects of desire
                maintain, obscurely, their entire
existence
        (because that's all the talk there is,
that which,
        (in its measureless insistence,
brings
    back to the beginningless completion
    of one's own unthinkable not-self
of things.

ENDING

to be not in
but at the limit of
the world
    moving & being moved
    only from another point of view;
    but from one's own, neither
    moving nor being moved
leaving all particulars of motion
up to passing days, not twice, with smile,
    (what the sages teach
is easy to find hard:

to be not in
but at the limits of
the world

is not to be in any place
that can be named beforehand,
& instruction how to go
is a kind of name beforehand:

but / a voice (& nothing more
    is seen
        in silences
    to questions that nobody asks,
    giving answers that nobody seeks
it stays, is fast,
    but, when the smile
    comes like an arm out of water
    & spreads out its fingers over your face;
    like a hollow reed
    comes, with flowering face,
follows.

(1956)

CANTICLES FOR THE HOURS: PRIME

1.

alive in the tissue of water, the round white light
is a nipple of stone in the sky.

                     real moon,
turn on the dust in the lightwell of water to music;
loosen the air into words that will break
    like the ice, making wonderful eyes
open like flowers up through the water, breaks.

       no.
       this is the moon made of paper
       that thinks like a mirror, & murmurs
       & turns, unfinished in beauty, & flies,
       shedding pictures, into the cage of the eye
       entire, the womb of its time,
       & hurts like laughter from women.

2.

love was plainer than air is, at night.
daylight will tighten the skin,
& stretch out the air into words;

but while the space between words is still dark
              in the cage of the eye, where design
remains,)
poem, remind like a mirror.

no,
mirrors remind me of nights,
& ask me if I am afraid.

I look for myself in the mirrors,
reply,   I know
               about love, passing
               back & forth, a sound
               between the bodies;
               is kindled like music,
               grows into speech,
               is caged like a word, & waits,
               pacing, in sleep, knowing;
I know, yes,
I am afraid.

3.

nighttime reminds me of mirrors,
asking what is it the meanwhile
body did while it dreamed.

unable to say,
that it danced:

it squatted, &
it crouched,
&
three times I heard it say
         "come back."

squatted once upon haunches;
down-facing,
earth-regarding;
to living lover said,
come back

(at which the eye of the earth

looked reproachfully up)

crouched next upon buttocks;
upward-facing,
sky-regarding;   said
to object not desired but there,
come back

(which the ear of the sky heard,
unperturbed)

squatted the third time anyhow
squatted, huddled
in the empty water, pled
only for wanting to want,
come back

(which time's enormous mouth
was seen to smile at, swallowing

come back,   *come back,*   *come back*

& let the triple world
be shaken like a wing
as we lean together on the centre of the air
& dance, & sing

4.

only the morning comes back
the radial hair of the sun streaming in,
thick & terribly straight, sweeping the cage.

     look at the moon, how it fades
all day like a mirror that thinks

& remembers, filling the earth,
& slows it.

    soon the real body quickens & wakes.
I love you.   lie still.

                is what death is,
                a coming back, a
                filling of the eye,
                a clearing out;
                is what death is,
                & echoes do;
                is design.

THREAD

next,
'in the seventh generation, cease
                the orderly arrangement of your songs
                              the words

remind us not to be in love with corpses,

    carried in the whirlpool like a dance,
    a spell where numbers of the other   swimmers change to strings
    of   (disappear in language)   words to follow from word to word
    although the stretch is trackless where the numbers were
        already caught, cut, to fit   impossible
        equations, & construct a world toward which
            to learn to face / to lift a face
        toward call it a river for flowing
        riverlike speech
                    a voice, or, watch, a play of voices

  because it is not death that language loves,
                but common waking after sleep;
as thought, as a breath, like a sail
            takes the wind   seaward
        out from edges of the world
           (with human speech so rare a thing
we have to make it up)   inventing an order, or finding
in foam, even in steam, mostly in ice, crystal, in skeletons, order;
in ice, skeletons

    or take a whole mountain, most
    is underwater, but take its name from what sticks up

    & icebergs as they melt: neither like a man
        who almost not thinking   floats
        in shallows, at midday   the warm body
        buoyant, or   as if sinking, not knowing
        that someone has straightened the bedclothes, falling asleep.

        ; nor not :

   where a skeleton in ice remains if it does,
  where a missing child's inside a closet would have kept on turning,

    'But it was only a movie, dear.'

'Everything,' said Thales. *He knew.*

& next   to know love as unconditioned reflex of the chaos that is there,

which is neither order nor disorder,"
   thus the thread of the water   *until it comes to*
    "neither heat nor cold, but their dissolution
       call compassion.

31.I.59

1.

because it wasn't sugar
but (a word i've found again surprise;
& again the need to begin
in words that leave no extra taste against the

   silence

  is a word for meeting,
  to make a horn out of gold & think of kind kings
  clearing the mud of that
       river, those
          clouds

  (what
if a man gets his knowledge from nowhere else
can he give as a name to his own

      mind, or

       never dissolved, by water,
drifts on the river's stone bottom
like shreds of raw silk
       seeming to waken
(because this water is not still)
the sheet-glass surface is quietly shaken
& breaks into ripples, as gulls rise
into the rooms of the hungry children
to watch the tall water close over their heads.

2.

well, old honey, back to the hard sound.
(what's keeping you?)

i think you want it too much too
somewhere as it is between the thorough
lawfulness of beehives, & on the other hand
this spiderweb that only seems to be a figure in a plane
is central: an extension of the sense of touch.

       but think of the spider as.   in its own web trapped
       (if any circumstance escapes yr notice
       i am sure to be there to show you
       nothing is going to happen
       in this waste of sand, yr desert of
       lapwings, or
       flights of accidental
       birds that cast such shadows toward the ground upon which
       this is yr life, neither
       here nor there,
       this is yr life, neither
       birds that cast such shadows toward the ground upon which
       flights of accidental
       lapwings, or
       in this waste of sand, yr desert of
       nothing is going to happen.

                              this matter, yr
              everyday life. because yes
              those forces were dangerous,
              & this trap that we wd like to call a poem, then,
              is not: the balance is yet to be struck
              toward which, trapped in this web,

which is not a figure in a plane. look again. begin to see it
as a tunnel.

3.

or say that it is not love
but a secret that opens toward waking
forms out of words escaping into the morning
that force us to go looking after.

are you not hearing out of another
room of the house such laughter as if
              we were children, making a game of the law

        & this action, a going, a
          doing, a making
                        to come into being
           is a game, a dance, is
                         Lila
          (the play where the law stays, is fast)

is the hard part you missed
is the stone that you wished such light out of water through clouds.

26.I.59

BRUCE BOYD

PART III

PART III

INTRODUCTION

I become tired of repeating static designs of the same names.

It is good to bring a real thing into a poem, so that something from the world a man has to live returns to him there. But making poems will not satisfy the kind of poetry that demands to come to the *particular* & real. It may be, to the *too* particular; but the hang-up that isn't the rejection of these particular though not less poetical desiderations (tired because the invitation of prolonged blank walls is more inhuman thought not, perhaps, less kind than the rim of light around a real & definite closed door) conjures up a troubled spirit, hungry ghost, that was a stillborn poem from being too unique, although a kind of angel too; & from possession by such particular beauty as will not even correspond to a closed door into the world, the poet turns exorcist. His poetry may otherwise *contain* real things, but it will never *enter* them.

The exorcist thinks twisty thoughts, means to twist those blank walls around into a blind alley. Any appearance of doors is not coincidental, which is to say miraculous, & the poet, failing that, has to turn around & not look back, for love, till anyone there turns on to a going street where his thoughts again can straighten out along his life & learn to know the difference between a root & branches, if there is one.

In the poem, the act, from its completion, carries to its preconditions a tension. What is needed is a bridge, to be the difference between a group & a community. Failing such a bridge comes the exorcists, & build a blind alley. What he says may not be a poem, but runs along briskly & can doubtless entertain in lower places than it enters the world like a dream-from-above, shallow, as it were, a metapoem, made to free the appetite for peaceful will a person serves.

It is good to bring a real thing into a poem. But the test of poems like the test of drugs is just their human use. A poem contains something real just to help the poem come into the real. To help.

There is a receptacle for pomegranate seeds at the first through left-hand turning.

PROEM

Narcissus, a little stone, a handful of pebbles, make waves;
I didn't go to do it, but the house
more fragile than glass, flickers & goes out

                                    comes back
as mercifully as possible
when there's nothing more to be shed. not at all like fire,
which is what a heated fuel   shed to keep its balance in the air;
& not remorse at being oneself: it is more instant, a more lasting
structure of despair, or fear; thus love is more appealing,
sometimes, through an eerie innocence of intellect
than through the eye
                why those herds of reindeer
were altogether elsewhere
& why that bird was tied, & fluttered everywhere
then settled onto its perch, like the mind
settles down on its life, it says in the Upanishad,
& sometimes a poem   comes home to roost,
as you agreed

      & it is right,
all these returns, because we keep on changing
not by our choice but our consent, is all,
yes.

TOWARD MORNING
(SOME APOTROPEIA INSTEAD OF AN ALBA)

where is the bitter taste I still don't taste
the famous biter taste. the many little pieces settled
in the empty stomach just as easily as pebbles, or balls
dropped from a tower

              quietly.   the smartest white horse
in your whole heaven is about to refuse to be put
through his paces more than
                    one mo' time,
listen to him stamp his foot
in a rhythm of old music/

   song, soft song

   in thinking that in making something mustn't happen
   is a poverty of satisfaction hard to lift:
   but above the flow of language is a world that makes it rise

              as Plato said to each
              a procession of his own

& it wasn't you I think of when I saw the moon or see the sun, —
but closer; where the tide comes

thus children, wading,
think they make it rise by moving back:
the magic is a law that sees to their advantage
in a tide, fullness of meaning in their moving
guiding (, Plato,)   the rising & falling

calling
      (the tide rising, the night   falling

the children back to the fire where food is

      (marshmallows, yes, they're   roasted

       & blankets under the stars
       spread   after the singing
       sleep until morning

in a rhythm of old music/   Washington's Monument or is it a posey
from Washington Square flickers in the center of the Altar of Heaven
as a million Chinamen enter, dressed as Uncle Sam; but somewhere a band
plays *Tall Paul*   (more than a roach is needed to help this music along)
& we fade to a view of the Great Wall of Canada, its reconstruction
being inspected by all of the Justices of the Supreme Court, foreground in
pigtails wearing gowns with dragon sleeves while another band is playing
Shīna no Yōrū, familiar to the Justices as *She Ain't Got No Yo-Yo*;
They are the Nine Muses; it is the same band/

   song, firm song

   in thinking that in making something mustn't happen
   is a poverty of satisfaction hard to lift:
   but above the flow of language is a world that makes it rise

       spring, brook, streaming river
   the whole analogy   complete in an ocean with tides & a moon,
       but where is a blue boat?

   it wobbles in the water, tied   to the brink of the river bed
   & no one is in it, but rats on the bank
   gnawing, & bird in their trees whose laughter
   brays in all the places where the bitten strands are severed

   & no one is in it, how lovely it will move until a wave

it is the same band/   that we now see dispersing
alarmed Lombards while the Statue of Liberty arrives at Rome to be crowned.
palanquins, balustrades, apses, naves, & baldachins;   everyone
dressed in raiment. (right under our feet is a whole cellar of wines
guaranteed not to dirty the chalice.) this is the moment
the crown has been placed on her head: listen: as she sweetly smiles
at Holy Father & murmurs "filioque," he smiles brightly in return

& replies "just fine, thank you, & you?" & the Trapp Family Singers
open a set with *Vivat in Aeternum*, as a great shout escapes the crowd of farmers
& most of the poor people of Paris France assembled in the square outside
are only there to kill the time till their inevitable bicycles
come along to dare them

                      & they will respond, or will they respond
with lists of the best 5 per cent. preferred stock, "look at our lists,
thou sluggard," irrelevantly,

           (the Christians need these buttons,
Kwannon send them laws)
               yes what I say, what I said, is personal,
was private, as all life that isn't shared *is* personal, is private,
& it's this that cancels out your definitions,
not being afraid to speak, I mean not speaking like you Christians
whose systems are a strident shriek
that makes the good/

    song, hard song

in thinking that in making something mustn't happen

        the actual act, as if it meant one thing.
        the honest word, as if we knew it,

is a poverty of satisfaction hard to life,

        as if it mattered.   like a pain in the ass
        you talk about your cock as if language were another
        Polk or Market Street, where a faggot will talk
        with his eyes, & what he says doesn't matter.

    but above the flow of language is a world that makes it rise,

that makes the good/   prefer the Jews, they made a god they can rebuke
because they know he loves them, or like we Buddhists have our self-respect,
a proper pride, although we grant you the position is absurd;   while
you Christians have your little lists & congregations of the 5 per cent.,

the self-elect;   which shows that what you love is only language (& "this
air severe is but a mere veneer," sir,
                              not what language is about.
But there's even a Buddha that smiles
at honest fakes; his angels know that what it means
is that the world those poems that we see around us
has got an equal brilliance with out minds, is all;
& waits to be born in the bodies of men

                         while you poor Christians think
you have to build your dirty earth right here in heaven,
here in heaven where your poverty of mind is out of place,
that you actually have
to imagine

    inside this room with its enormous focused butterflies
    water & clouds & canyons of millions of little wax candles

WE INTERRUPT THIS BROADCAST TO TEACH YOU IF YOU CAN'T
MAKE IT IN THIS WORLD AT LEAST RESPECT SAME

                              Respect?
yes that world *should* make you laugh, because it means that someone else
is thinking you're the cornballs, & little ones upon their backs, laugh,
& giants, to bite 'em, & this too shall, & so on, grandfathers die first,
& you are old enough, I think,

        Pygmalion, had a skeleton
    in his closet, knew
    it is because the posture
    of those bones was lovely,
    that they should be immortalized in flesh

because you may not know what time it is, this moment, in time
is one you won't forget, not even if you think
of everything it could have meant, & there's still
time, moments are like that, until the next

WAR

oh well, we angels try, is all:
if they won't come to terms we follow
them into the music.   where we have to stop when it does,
all the time.

Anthems of All of the Nations. Would you like to hear that band again?

                (Or the 36th Section, beginning
                "The Buddha said, it is hard . . .
                to be born a human being.")

Now then. There is someone in this room who never answers any questions.
All the rest of you should leave whenever you think you're being cheated.
Excuse me.

     — *he'll never get away! Spider,   can't stand 'em, spiders
eat snakes* —

          whenever you think you're being cheated.   Now then.
"Fool," you say, "fool."   "He's a fool," you say;   &, *he's* a fool, you say,
yes

    everything is food, we fetch it from the store & cook it on our stoves
at home in pots.   but *our* China serves up more than just the words
for our infusions,
             interfusion,
                    synaesthesia,
community, no that's not it either, not communion,

                        but we might as well scarf,
I'll make some waffles, with Bisquick, it's so easy,
                          & meanwhile
under the bridge,
        "like I think I hear your mother coming calling sonny
        maybe you better go home"
                      (but he really wants

to stay kids, guess he will some time? no?   no guts?   he's just bugged
behind those feathers, at the end of his pen

              all the time, "fool,"
you say.   I never met the man who taught to use that word so much but then
the put-down prior is the clever coward's best defense

                  (like the next war,
man, with things like that to keep them cool these dirtmen still aren't
straightened out on politics,
        & all the time that you say fool the question
really is which one is the better fool, & when not in Rome which one seems
most nearly like a man without being simply counterfeit, & would not
                    do

in heaven
   wrongly, as the Romans do

then, now, for a long time, as

       in the field of this pure white departure
the field white furrowed blue to follow a line
             like a river, lit black
toward which all other colors flow between to draw the rhythm of its dance
in n-dimensional calligraphies, flow toward the light
           places, where the good
cities wait,

  or are we talking to ourselves, then?
  or like sometimes people take off all their clothes
    (something one does to be sure one isn't afraid, perhaps,
     (or the same thing when, one isn't afraid

look, those feathers on your pen, all you have to do to straighten them, is fly

so quo vadis, motherfucker?

       where will that coward in his cups
& gold of words go not to join to such melisma of the

                                        real it is in heaven
perhaps you just can't hear it here
                    on
                        how odd, we also call our heaven "Earth,'
where us angels sing all day (& that white horse, listen to it stamp its foot
just one mo' time) & night
                & our bon ami
                                hasn't scratched yet, but still
"how sad" is also a beginning, first flight;   & what was it we were saying
a hundred years ago?   something like
                        "a good boy sanctifies any cause," or
was that another music?   oh well, the war is dead, but we've had a lovely
trip,
    we've gone around the world
                        ("next year we go somepless else")
& you'll be caught with that same
                        you instead, one night, once more, you might

say what it is you've got a mouth for that you talk to with, if you've
got any eyes at all, because next morning no one's going to ask "are you
still carrying that girl," that swan or was it just a duck, a plaster
duck (pillow-words rise blushing to take their bows, their original, golden
vows
nemi
nemo
no one's going to ask, am I still carrying that girl, that swan that bear

that boy that monkey —
                    money wouldn't drive the changers from his temple
on my back

        I left you by the river
        dance, lover, closer, if you can
                                or lovely even if you
                                        now the sun
or whatever it is, comes up, that they'll call it

>   (don't you want to bet?   *sure* you want to bet,
>   (I mean you up there, in your rosey-fingered bleachers)
>
>   or swim if you find
>   above the rise of language, tread
>   a world to make it flow,
>   we can

like where do you really want to go?   isn't the boat?   the cargo was swamped, or gone aground

in thinking that in making something mustn't happen,

or to-morrows sun, another turning couldn't listen later
if we called come back, but offer better
things to do than fuck a duck darkly or swim
if you can, till birds like you
can sing in the sun they'd better not dance
until they must;   or if the sun says its either
you or they (for the sun is both, but
which you are is either) or if you can
where the end of the thread climbs risers & treads
                                point the way to waltz
>   inside the brightest ballroom of the mind:
>   I watch how the walls twist somehow away toward the cities.

ENVOY, WITH ANGELIC ORDERS

a poem, a group of poems

a poem, a group of poems, a poem about a group of poems;

a community of poems: a poem,

    & it's not enough to only look at rainbows,
    but if this much came out of your silence, only
    think, what if we should speak

    you shouldn't complain
                                it's you who've said nothing
        only one person
                        speaks, as a rule,
            at a time

        Narcissus cross the river,
        I have just gone away,

look here, your Buddha-Nature wants you to write
me a poem again & do what the poem will say.

CHRONOLOGICAL ORDER OF PUBLICATION

Evergreen Review, edited by Barney Rosset and Donald Allen. Vol. 2, No. 6, Autumn, 1958. "Aubade"

J: A Magazine of Poetry. Issue No. 1 (1959, edited by George Stanley "After Midnight." Issue No. 3 (1959), edited by George Stanley. "Introduction"; "Proem"; "Toward Morning (Some Apotropeia Instead of an Alba); "Envoy, with Angelic Orders"

The New American Poetry, edited by Donald Allen (New York: Grove Press, 1960). "This Is What the Watchbird Sings, Who Perches in the Tree"; "Venice Recalled"; "Sanctuary"

The Floating Bear: a newsletter. Issue 15 (1961), edited by Amiri Baraka, Diane Di Prima. "Canticles for the Hours: Prime"; "Thread" Parts 1, 2, and 3. "

Yugen, edited by Amiri Baraka and Hettie Cohen. Issue 7 (1961). "Summer Nightmusic"; "This is How the Wind Sings, Lover, On the Beach"; "A Quarrel of Minstrels"; "Water"; "Song"; & "Poem"

Mendicant, edited by William Margolis. Issue No. 1. "Flowerpot Sutra"; "Scratching"

12 Poets and 1 Painter (book) — Donald Allen. Four Seasons Foundation, 1964. "N O W"

"Venice Recalled" was reprinted in Bill Mohr's *Holdouts: The Los Angeles Poetry Renaissance* (University of Iowa Press, 2011); "Venice Recalled" was also reprinted, along with "Sanctuary," "What the Watchbird Sings, Who Perches in the Lovetree," and "N O W," in *Cross-Strokes: Poetry between Los Angeles and San Francisco*, edited by Bill Mohr and Neeli Cherkovski (Seismicity Editions/Otis College of Art and Design, 2015.

NOTE ON THE EDITOR

Bill Mohr is a professor emeritus at California State University, Long Beach, where he has taught since 2006, after receiving his Ph.D. in Literature from the University of California, San Diego in 2004. In 2011, the University of Iowa Press published *Hold-Outs: The Los Angeles Poetry Renaissance 1948-1992*. His reviews, articles, and commentary have also appeared in the *Bloomsbury Handbook of Contemporary American Poetry*, *Poetry Flash*, *Journal of Beat Studies*, *Chicago Review*, *William Carlos Williams Review*, *Poetry Project Newsletter*, *Hungry Mind Review*, *New Review of Literature*, *OR*, *Los Angeles Review of Books*, *Los Angeles Times*, and *Beyond Baroque NEW*.

Mohr has a chapter on L.A. poetry forthcoming in a volume entitled "L.A.: A Literary History" from Cambridge University Press in 2026 as well as an essay forthcoming in a CUP volume celebrating the centenary of Allen Ginsberg's birth. Prior to his career as an academic, Mohr made his living at various occupations, including working as a blueprint machine operator and typesetter. During this time, he was the editor and publisher of Momentum Press, which he founded in 1974 (www.koankinship.com)

In addition to being translated into Spanish, Italian, Croatian, and Japanese, Mohr's poems have appeared in over 20 anthologies. Mohr's most recent full-length collection of poems is a bilingual edition, *The Headwaters of Nirvana / Los Manantiales del Nirvana* (What Books, Los Angeles, 2018). What Books will publish *Remiges: Collected Longer Poems* in the fall 2026.

Mohr has been a visiting scholar at the Getty Research Institute and been honored with Beyond Baroque's George Drury Smith Award. His literary and editorial archives are at the Archive for New Poetry in the Special Collections Library at the University of California, San Diego.

Mohr wishes to acknowledge the assistance of several RSCA (Research, Scholarly, and Creative Activity) awards and three sabbaticals from California State University Long Beach which either directly or indirectly assisted with the compilation of this book.

www.ingramcontent.com/pod-product-compliance
Lightning Source LLC
LaVergne TN
LVHW041633070526
838199LV00052B/3328